THE
Archive Photographs
SERIES

LLANDAFF

Print of the west front of Llandaff Cathedral, sold in aid of the Victorian restoration.

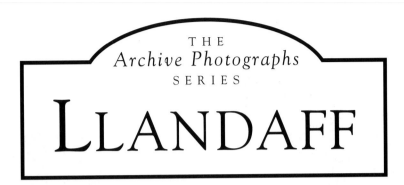

THE
Archive Photographs
SERIES

LLANDAFF

Compiled by
The Llandaff Society
Cymdeithas Llandaf

CHALFORD

First published 1996
Copyright © The Llandaff Society Cymdeithas Llandaf, 1996

The Chalford Publishing Company
St Mary's Mill, Chalford,
Stroud, Gloucestershire, GL6 8NX

ISBN 0 7524 0380 X

Typesetting and origination by
The Chalford Publishing Company
Printed in Great Britain by
Redwood Books, Trowbridge

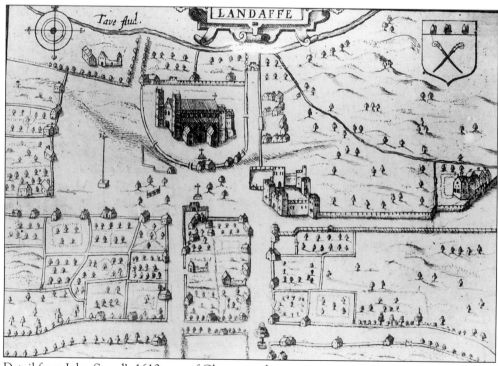

Detail from John Speed's 1610 map of Glamorganshyre.

4

Contents

Llandaff corn mill, prior to its demolition in the 1930s.

Introduction

By Matthew Williams, Keeper of the Collections, Cardiff Castle.

Old photographs can stir and evoke our memories in an unique and powerful way. Those from the distant past delight our imagination, whilst more recent images make us aware of how people and places are subtly changed by each succeeding year.

Llandaff, with its ancient Cathedral and dignified Green, seems fixed in our minds as permanent and largely unchanging. Yet the images in this book demonstrate how relentless is the process of change, and how, within the space of a lifetime, the face of Llandaff has altered, sometimes beyond recognition.

Fascinating as all of these photographs are, it is the very early views, those that date from the middle of the last century, that provide perhaps the greatest revelation. Luckily for us, the early days of photography just managed to capture the old Llandaff, as it had existed for centuries, with ancient houses and low huddles of traditional white painted, thatched cottages set amid the muddy roadways.

The nineteenth century completely transformed Llandaff from a neglected backwater into a prosperous and worldly community, and the camera was there to record the changes. The range of photographs of The Green illustrate the transformation, and although for some years humble cottages sat cheek by jowl with smarter and more affluent neighbours, they gradually disappeared for ever. Some photographs, such as those of thatched cottages in High Street in 1898, actually show the sad process of demolition. From the late 1850s, perhaps attracted by the healthy rural situation of Llandaff, and by the great revival of its Cathedral, industrial barons, made wealthy by the coal and shipping boom in Cardiff, moved into the district. Pasture land was given up to Gothic and neo-Tudor mansions in extensive grounds, and gradually Llandaff lost its isolation from Cardiff and became linked by roads lined with prosperous houses. The restored Cathedral, now with an active, resident clergy, lent a dignity to the City that was quite absent a century before, and new educational institutions were encouraged to settle in Llandaff.

Despite this new found dignity, Llandaff, unlike many cathedral cities, managed to retain its village atmosphere, and this is so well conveyed in the photographs that show the little pubs, shops, the school groups and the lively village outings. Perhaps it is the physical siting of the Cathedral itself, set low in a hollow, imposing, but without being pompous or dominant, that accounts for an overall lack of pretension.

The twentieth century brought about immense change to Llandaff, as it did everywhere else. The population increased greatly, and as the century progressed, patterns of work and play changed. The photos of Edwardian Llandaff are evocative of a way of life that has disappeared for ever, sweeping away old certainties for some, hardship and disease for others. The appearance of the motor car around the turn of the century, heralded perhaps the greatest instrument of change, and gradually between the two world wars the population became increasingly mobile. With the car came the need for new and wider roads, and familiar buildings such as Llandaff Mill, and favourite walks, were swallowed up by the new Western Avenue, which cut a swathe through the district in the early thirties. The Victorian estates too, began to disappear beneath the avenues, closes and walks of semi-detached houses, a process which accelerated in the years following the end of the Second World War. The war itself brought the near destruction of the Cathedral, and the photographs of the disastrous land-mine damage of 1941 make the post-war restoration seem all the more remarkable.

The second half of the twentieth century has seen the disappearance of some well-loved landmarks, although thankfully, Llandaff has suffered less than many other places from the enthusiasm of the post-war planner. Even so, losses such as the historic Cathedral School on The Green, and the Victorian village school in High Street are remembered with regret. Today soon becomes yesterday, and images of Llandaff in the 1950s seem as remote to the younger generation as those of the Victorian village are to their elders.

A village feeling still persists today, however, and High Street bustles with activity, although the greengrocers and butchers have given way to building societies and banks, while shops beyond High Street have disappeared altogether.

The twentieth century is the first to be captured complete by the camera lens. How appropriate therefore, as we approach the Millennium, that the Civic Society's 'Llandaff 2000' project will photograph the Llandaff of today, for tomorrow's social historian. The last twenty years have witnessed a general revival of interest in our architectural heritage, and thanks to the efforts of the Llandaff Society, we have all been made more aware of our 'village' - past and present.

Llandaff High Street, 1898. The thatcher is commencing the removal of the roof prior to the demolition of the cottages next to the Black Lion.

One

Approaches to Llandaff

Set on a small plateau of Triassic sandstone between the flood plains of the rivers Taff and Ely, Llandaff stands at the intersection of at least two ancient roads. The Romans' north-south route from the Llantrisant iron mines to the sea came up Bridge Street, across The Green and down Court Lane alongside the Castle, rejoining the line of the present Cardiff Road beyond Mill Lane, and on down Penhill and Llandaff Road. Travelling east to west, the principal Roman road is thought to have passed well to the north of the fort at Cardiff, crossing the Taff near the present Cathedral and continuing down the line of High Street and Ely Road.

We can only conjecture what led the saints to choose this location for their church some time around AD 560. Pre-Christian burials discovered under the north-west tower indicate that it may already have been a sacred site. It was certainly sheltered from sea raiders, though accessible on the tide, and also marked the lowest point where the Taff could conveniently be forded. From the Middle Ages or earlier the routes now known as Pwllmelin and Fairwater roads, converging a quarter of a mile from their target, will have carried pilgrims from the Border Vale to the shrines of the saints. The way led along Heol Fair, where Black Hall and St Mary's probably offered hospitality, and down the hill to the Cathedral Church. Speed's map of 1610 shows that The Green in his day was very much larger than it is now, and also indicates the importance of the roads north-south and down to the River Taff. The path across Llandaff Fields from Pontcanna was a popular way for Victorians to approach Llandaff, particularly after Cathedral Road had been built. Much of the charm of this walk has since been lost, however, and the thrusting of Western Avenue - the 'orbital road' - through Llandaff in the early 1930s has meant that any attempt to reach the old city on foot carries the considerable risk of crossing the traffic-laden A4119 or A48.

Llandaff Fields, viewed from the south-east, c. 1912. This land was secured by covenant for the community in 1898, having long been a popular place of recreation for families of all classes. On the right is Llandaff corn mill. With Pontcanna still within the Parish of Llandaff, the walk north-west across the fields was the most direct and level, as well as the most agreeable, route to the Cathedral. The drinking fountain, just visible on the extreme left, is said to have been placed there at the initiative of Mrs Herbert Thompson of Whitley Batch; she had sat in her window watching the poor families from Grangetown who came to the fields for the day carrying bottles of water, and wished to make things easier for them.

Nearer the Cathedral, 1906. On the left is the Bishop's Field while the Mill Pond, to the right, is just out of sight. The cemetery visible in the right background had been established in 1884 on land rented from the Ecclesiastical Commissioners by Mr Clement Waldron. He retained the garden on the left, which was then given a good wall, by which he considered 'the approach to the Cathedral by the fields much improved'. The kissing gate was one of three on this footpath which were removed in the 1970s to allow pushchairs to pass more easily. The ruined Bishop's Castle can be seen on the escarpment at the extreme left of the picture with Well Cottage below it and Cathedral Cottage further down the hill.

Fairwater in the 1930s, from the west. The road to Llandaff leads round to the left (the direction the car appears to be going) in front of Brook Farm, beyond which Fairwater Road turns right and passes Fairwater House (visible on the right through the trees). This was the home of Major Evan David whose father, also Evan David, lived in a house out of sight to the left of the picture, which after his death became the Reardon Smith Nautical College. The sign post on the extreme right, which can still be seen, though in a different position, was cast at the Eagle Foundry by Mr Evans (see page 61).

Fairwater Road, early 1890s. Fairwater Road joins with Pwllmelin Road, on the right, to lead to Llandaff. This ancient route between Llandaff and the Vale would have carried pilgrims to and from Llancarfan and Llantwit Major. Until the intensive residential development of the 1950s and 1960s, Pwllmelin Road, once it had crossed the Taff Vale Railway, had open country on both sides, including a lane regularly used as a gypsy campsite.

View from the north, c. 1860 showing the turnpike gates at the junction of Llantrisant Road on the left and Bridge Road on the right. Visible on the extreme right are the Strawberry Fields and cottage.

The Mill Stream and the Arls Field, *c.* 1900. The path on the left is traditionally the route by which bodies were brought from Whitchurch to Llandaff before the 'White Church' had a burial ground, and was therefore known as 'Ffordd y Meirw' (Road of the Dead). The Mill Stream is crossed here by an iron bridge ideally suited to the pastime of 'Pooh sticks'; on the far side the Arls Field has not yet been laid out in the allotments it contained until the Mill Stream was drained and building of Llandaff Technical College began in 1952. No trace of the ruins of the Archdeacon's Castle can be seen, unless the ridges on the extreme right of the picture can be so identified. Although already shown as ruined in 1610, Clement Waldron wrote in 1895 that this building was in use as a cow house by Mr Huckwell the Registrar 'some forty years ago'.

Route from the south, *c.* 1900. Approaching from Cardiff, the Llandaff horse-bus would travel up Llandaff Road to Penhill and along Cardiff Road to High Street. Here it moves in the opposite direction along Romilly Crescent, passing the Llandaff School for the Deaf and Dumb, which had moved from Landscape Place in Bridge Street, Llandaff in 1865.

Two

The City

Llandaff has never been a pretentious city, even in the heyday of pilgrimages and votive offerings, and disendowment under Henry VIII set it on a downward course. The Civil War brought further damage to the fabric itself, which absentee bishops did nothing to mend, and one can picture the 'mean streets' of seventeenth and eighteenth century Llandaff lined with humble cottages fronted by pigsties notable to the nose as well as the eye. Since about 1265, when the Bishop (probably William de Brewsa) set his fortified palace strategically on the escarpment, few fine houses had been built, and some of these had fallen into ruin. A tourist of 1803 experienced 'considerable surprise and disappointment' at the contrast with finer (and cleaner) English cathedral cities. Even the gaiety of the Whitsun fair deteriorated into squalor and violence and, its primary functions having disappeared, the fair was suppressed in 1880. The great Victorian revival, reflecting as it did the increasing prosperity of neighbouring Cardiff and the energy and devotion of the first Bishop and Dean to be resident in centuries, transformed the scene. The architects John Prichard and Ewan Christian pioneered the building of a new Llandaff which, supplemented by more recent developments, we now inherit. Green fields and large gardens have been lost and a sad number of handsome trees felled, but the city is still viewed as 'a favourite residence for the money getting people of Cardiff' and is watched over as a conservation area.

LLANDAFF CATHEDRAL, NR. CARDIFF.

Approaching the City, c. 1930. Across the path from Llandaff Fields can be seen, on the left, the Cathedral School pavilion. Above it is Well Cottage and to the right The White House. Below The White House is Cathedral Cottage and the pine-end of another earlier cottage. The hedge in the foreground divided the Bishop's Field from the Cathedral School playing field.

Insole Cottages. Nos 98-104 Cardiff Road were originally built by the Insole family of Insole Court for their employees, but were demolished in 1933 when Western Avenue was built. No 98 was occupied by Mr and Mrs Pearce, No 100 by Miss Smith who took in washing, No 102 by Mr Rolf, and No 104 by Bill Grills. Bill worked for William Clarke's, the sculptors, from about 1895. During the First World War he worked as a gardener to Mr Thompson at 'Whitley Batch', but returned to Clarke's after the war. His son, Melvyn carried on the family tradition of working for Clarke's. Bill died c. 1968.

Before the building of Western Avenue, c. 1930. William Clarke's original offices and yard, with girls from Howell's School waiting for a bus at what was then the end of Palace Road.

William Clarke's new offices decorated for the coronation of King George VI on 12 May 1937. In the foreground is the new roundabout, the first to appear in Cardiff, at the junction of Western Avenue and Cardiff Road.

The lodge of the former Bishop's Palace, 1976. This building was demolished in 1976 to allow for the widening of Cardiff Road at its junction with Western Avenue. As for the Palace itself, the architect is unknown but is traditionally supposed to have been John Wood the Elder of Bath. The lodge building, although picturesque, offered a poor standard of accommodation with small rooms and no modern services.

Llandaff Court. Built in 1744-46 as a residence for Admiral Thomas Mathews - who never deigned to live there - it served as the Bishop's Palace (Llys Esgob) between 1850 and 1939. Following a serious fire in 1914, the roof and the upper floors were reconstructed. In 1958 it became the home of the Cathedral School.

The Bishop's Palace, pre-1914. To the left of the garden, at the front of the main building, a small chapel was built in 1858-59 by Ewan Christian. To the right at the bottom of the slope stood the dairy, in the well of which, in 1870, Bishop Ollivant uncovered the Celtic cross which now stands in the south choir aisle of the Cathedral.

Cardiff Road to the south-east. The building of the half-timbered house to the right, known formerly as Lletty Derw and now called Tudor House, is usually ascribed to George Halliday, a local architect. The low, tiled building to the left of it was demolished to make way for the construction of Palace Avenue and a terrace of new houses in Cardiff Road.

Cardiff Road, Llandaff.

Cardiff Road to the north-west. To the right of Lletty Derw is Primrose Cottage, still thatched, beyond which is St Michael's Theological College and the Maltsters Arms. During the First World War both St Michael's College and The Lodge (through the gateway to the right) were used as convalescent hospitals for wounded servicemen, some of whom can be seen seated outside the entrance to The Lodge.

Llandaff Probate Registry. Built between 1860 and 1863, this is arguably the best secular building designed by John Prichard, the restorer of Llandaff Cathedral in the mid-nineteenth century. It was constructed to meet the needs of the new civil probate administration which had been set up by the Court of Probate Act of 1857. Old Registry House, to the right, was also by Prichard and was designed to provide living accommodation for the Probate Registrar.

The Maltsters Arms, before its rebuilding, c. 1955. Standing on the corner of Ely Road and Cardiff Road, this is one of the oldest hostelries in Llandaff. Here can be seen the mounting block and a flight of steps leading to an upper room, below which was, and is, the cellar.

Junction of Cardiff Road and High Street, prior to the First World War. St Michael's College stands in the background on the right-hand side of the road, with cottages and sheds occupying the ground on which a red brick building was to arise later. To the left, the Black Lion had not yet been decorated with mock half-timbering.

Junction of Cardiff Road and High Street, between the wars. The Black Lion and its adjoining off-licence had, by this time, acquired their half-timbering and on the opposite corner the new red brick building had appeared with, at ground level, Hallett's the confectioner's and a chemist with domestic accommodation above. The ground floor and basement of this building is now occupied by the Midland Bank.

High Street, *c.* 1875. It is only in the last hundred years that High Street has become the main shopping centre in Llandaff. Known at one time as St Peter Street, it was mainly a residential area until the first school was built in 1855 (out of sight here), at the top of the street. This school housed the pupils who were formerly taught in the upper room of the Cathedral Chapter House. At this time there were thatched cottages on both sides of the lower end of the street, which was unsurfaced and flanked with open drains. John Prichard's new National school, built in 1867 to accommodate an increased school population, stood on the western side of High Street.

High Street, 12 March 1898. Demolition of the cottages at the lower end of High Street was caught here by the camera of Mr Jonas Watson, the timber-merchant who built 'The Lodge' in Cardiff Road. To the right of the demolished cottages the pine end of the Probate Registry can be seen.

Next door to the Maltsters Arms. A tablet over the doorway of this house bore the date 1807, and like the thatched cottage immediately to its right, it was demolished in 1958. The building at the extreme right was part of the stable block of 'The Hendre' which was demolished in 1959.

High Street, January 1935. This cottage on the corner of Cardiff Road and High Street was the first to be demolished to make way for road widening. To the left can be seen, on the other side of Cardiff Road, part of 'The Hendre' stable block.

High Street, Saturday, 4 July 1903. Viewed from an upper room in the Maltsters Arms, the 1st battalion of the Welsh Regiment come marching down High Street behind the regimental band with their mascot (the goat) at the head. This parade followed the dedication of two memorial brasses in the Cathedral commemorating those who fell in the Boer and South African wars.

William Evans, baker and grocer, born 1844. At first William baked his bread in the oven of No 2, Chapel Street while his new premises in High Street were being built. His uncle, David Evans, was Lord Mayor of London in 1891, and his brother's daughter was Clara Novello Davies, the mother of Ivor Novello. He was succeeded in the business by his son Tom who sold it in 1918 to Woods and Seig.

High Street. Small single-storied shops fronted two of the cottages on the western side of High Street: Miss Lewis's sweet shop and the lower Shepstone's butcher's shop (the lower of the two). Another branch of the Shepstone family also had a butcher's business at the upper end of High Street in what is now 'Town and Country'. Latterly, a cobbler occupied the third cottage.

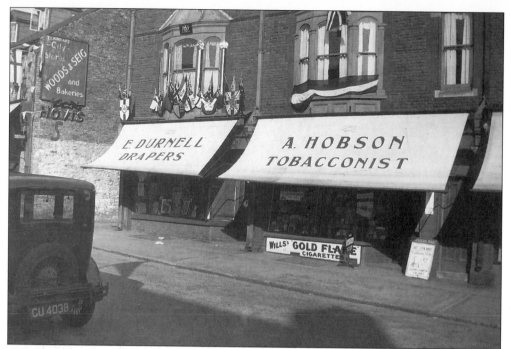

High Street, 12 May 1937. Two of the three-storied shops which replaced the thatched cottages (see page 20b) were decorated to celebrate the coronation of King George VI and Queen Elizabeth. Outside the newsagents, the 'Western Mail' billboard advertised its Coronation supplement. The premises of Woods and Seig, on the left, were subsequently demolished and the site is now occupied by the National Westminster Bank.

High Street. The hoardings which ran down the western side of High Street, gave way in the mid-1930s to a line of shops to the right of the picture. The Maltsters Arms faced up High Street and was almost totally rebuilt in 1957-8. A malting business had existed on the site as early as 1703.

The Green, *c.* 1860. Of the structures shown, only the Castle, the preaching cross and the wall of The White House remain. The thatched cottage to the right of the Castle is now the site of 'St Peblig' and 'St Bride' and the adjoining three-storied Tudor farmhouse was demolished in 1863 to be replaced by 'St Mary' on the corner of Heol Fair. The state of the road calls for no comment!

Coronation visit of King George V and Queen Mary, 26 June 1912. Bishop Pritchard Hughes accompanied the King, while Queen Mary was escorted by Canon James Rice Buckley.

The Green, *c.* 1920. Between the preaching cross and the Cathedral stood, surrounding the ancient campanile, the Red Lion Inn, later known as Tower House. To the right of Tower House can be seen the narrow entrance leading to the west front of the Cathedral. Beyond Tower House stood a grocer's shop which, in this photograph, was already in the course of demolition, revealing the pine end of 'The Cottage', now The Deanery.

The preaching cross. This marks the traditional site at which Giraldus Cambrensis (Gerald of Wales) and Archbishop Baldwin preached the Third Crusade in 1188. Only the lower third of the shaft and the stone into which it is set are original.

The Green, *c.* 1920. The grassed areas were enclosed with a neat post and chain surround as part of the general improvements made to The Green at the time of Queen Victoria's Diamond Jubilee in 1897 under the active leadership of Canon Buckley. As part of the same scheme the head of the preaching cross was turned by ninety degrees.

The Green, pre-1897. The thatched cottages on the left hand side of the Green behind the lime tree were superseded by the elegant three-storied tile-hung houses, Nos 7 to 13. Beyond all the cottages and the half-timbered house ('Cheverell') was the White Lion Inn.

27

The Green. Silhouetted, and in deep shadow, is the bronze figure of Archdeacon Buckley by Sir William Goscombe John. Buckley was Vicar of the parish of Llandaff from August 1878 until his death in 1924 - 'A man he was to all the country dear'. The building shown centrally was occupied by the Cathedral School from 1880 to 1958. Former known as Green Court, it was originally a two-storied building, an encroachment on The Green, and was occupied at one time by the widow of Dean William Bruce Knight. The cottage to its left provided accommodation for the headmaster. The building to the extreme right was built between 1861 and 1863 as a canonry to the design of Ewan Christian. It is now known as 'Pendinas'.

The Green, *c.* 1930. In the centre are the only two ancient cottages which remained on The Green with Bolt's Stores occupying the left hand one. 'Cheverell', to the right of the cottages, was built in 1888 for Mr Alexander Bassett by Halliday & Anderson.

The Green, pre-1924. The building almost hidden in the trees to the right of the Canonry was built by Ewan Christian as the Deanery. Having served as the Bishop's house between 1953 and 1988, it has since been converted into private flats and is known as Cathedral Court. The war memorial, which was dedicated in 1924, was executed by Sir William Goscombe John and erected at the furthest point of this grassed area of The Green.

Glass's Mews and Tower House. Viewed from the top end of The Green, the group of buildings at the centre were Glass's Mews where carriages might be hired and where dancing classes were held in an upper room. Immediately to the right of the mews stood Tower House.

Ffynnon Teilo. This ancient well in Cathedral Close is, by tradition, a site associated with St Teilo, one of the early bishops connected with Llandaff. It is certainly one of the many wells upon which Llandaff long relied for its drinking water. It has recently been refurbished and enclosed.

Cathedral Cottage, 1911. Almost at the foot of the hill in Cathedral Close stood Cathedral Cottage, which was so seriously damaged by the blast from the land mine which fell in the south churchyard on 2 January 1941 as to be beyond repair. The site is now occupied by 'Glenfield'. At the time this picture was taken Mr Rex, a gardener, and his family lived here.

Heol-y-Pavin (Pavement Street). Looking towards The Green, the first house on the right, now known as Rickyard Cottage, which together with No 11, Heol-y-Pavin was built by Thomas M. Maxfield. He was an assistant verger at the Cathedral for over thirty years and may be seen as the central figure here. At the far end of Heol-y-Pavin are the gabled roofs of the Alms Houses and beyond them the White Lion Inn.

The Alms Houses. This ancient building, which figures in the Hearth Tax assessment of 1670, was demolished, together with the adjacent White Lion Inn, at the end of the nineteenth century. The building to the right remains in use.

Bridge Street. Many of the cottages were replaced in the latter part of the nineteenth century, but traces of some of them can still be found behind the apparently Victorian façades. The more modern picture (below) shows Spencer's Terrace and the arched entrance to Spencer's Row at its centre. In 1877 a school, which was later to become the Cathedral School, was founded in No 32, Bridge Street, the double gabled house. The terrace of white cottages in the far distance was known as Somerset Place.

Archway to Spencer's Row. This terrace of cottages was built in 1866 by Messrs C. de Berque as workers' housing. The cottages were said to have been designed to accommodate lodgers as well as families. The arch was flanked by two shops: in the 1920s these were the grocer's shop of Miss Preston to the left and Miss Tucker's sweet shop to the right. It is believed that this is the sweet shop immortalised by Roald Dahl in *Boy*. More recently the shops have been Spiro's Delicatessen and Mr Wiggin's hardware; both have lately been converted to residential use.

Lower Bridge Street. At one time the Dean and Chapter owned the freehold of the land on which The Mitre stood, which possibly accounts for its name. When the pub became redundant, the land was developed for housing. Beyond the turning to Mitre Place are the houses known as Landscape Place and beyond them Siluria Terrace, which includes The Heathcock. The two houses at the left hand side are on the site of the old Toll House.

The Wesleyan Methodist chapel on Cardiff Road, 1898. In the latter part of the nineteenth century Llandaff had two chapels. The other congregation was that of the Calvinistic Methodists in Chapel Street. The Wesleyan Methodists are shown here about to embark for their Whitsun treat from their chapel in Cardiff Road south of its junction with Heol Fair. The photograph, below, shows the party at the treat. Edward Jones, later to become Deputy Chairman of SWEB, can be seen wearing a sailor hat and sitting on his father's lap in the second row.

'The Hendre'. This Georgian house, extensively enlarged and altered, faced directly onto Cardiff Road. It was occupied continuously by members of the David family for over a hundred years until it was requisitioned for military use during the Second World War. It was here that Edward David, together with Evan David who lived at Fairwater House, kept rainfall and temperature records for many years during the nineteenth century. These records show that summer temperatures were higher than those experienced a century later and that there was considerably more rain. The harvest period of 1848, for example, was catastrophically wet! After the Second World War, the house was acquired by Cardiff City Council as an old people's residential home, and an extension wing appeared to the left of the garden front of the house. The old house was demolished in 1959 but a desire to save the magnificent magnolias resulted in the retention of part of the shell of the building, which can be seen today.

Stable block, Llandaff House. For some years this was occupied by Boswell's building yard and Gould's the cobbler. A weather-vane which graced the roof was removed in the 1940s after war damage. The building itself was demolished and replaced with a modern office block in the 1970s. Access to the yard was through an arched entrance, with stairs to the upper floor from within the arch.

Llandaff Mews, Ely Road. Now the site of the entrance to Cranmer Court, this building was formerly the Greyhound Inn, and latterly, around 1918, was known as Llandaff Mews. Thomas James the blacksmith had his forge behind these premises in 1881.

Three

Early Days

'Two day and Sunday Schools, one whereof commenced 1825 contains 51 females; the other commenced 1829, 67 males', reported an enquiry of Llandaff in 1833. Child mortality was high at this time, not only during the dreadful cholera years of 1849 and 1854, and families were large. The little streets of Spencer's Row ('under the arch'), Heol-y-Pavin and Chapel Street were full of children, sometimes ten to a house (there was more than one reason why 'playing out' was desirable) and the street games of marbles, hoops, tops, skipping and tag kept them happy. During the First World War, though, the arrival of a telegraph boy would bring all street games to a standstill, while the children watched to see which house the boy would go to - and whose father would never be coming home.

To picture the life of children of late nineteenth and early twentieth century Llandaff one has to make two fundamental adjustments, namely to remove motor cars from the scene and set 'Mam' at home full time. Add the benign presence of several policemen in Bridge Street, and we were safe indeed. The roads were rough, but almost empty of all but horse-drawn vehicles. Playing out was universal. At fourteen most children were expected to go out to work to help the family budget, but there were still opportunities for having fun. The girls went dancing either at the Institute or Glass's Mews; the boys played football or fives. Miss Hughes, the Bishop's daughter, used to run a youth club called The Young Persons' Union in the basement of the Palace, and this was probably the forerunner of the Girls' Friendly Society (GFS) which she also organised. Scouts started c. 1910, and the Guides in about 1916. The Brownie Pack, with Violet Finnimore, one of the first four guides, as their Brown Owl, started in 1923. The swimming baths in Llandaff Fields became a great summer attraction in the 1920s, and after the Second World War there was a fine flowering of Cymry'r Groes and other dramatic activity in which the whole community joined.

The striking contrast with conditions today was the freedom of movement enjoyed by children as individuals and the absence of the need for expensive equipment before you could enjoy yourself. One did not travel far, except for Whitsun treats or to visit relatives, but a child could set off for school or Sunday school alone on foot or by bicycle as a matter of course and return safely. Adventures climbing trees or playing by the river supplemented football, cricket or tag; the fun fair at Barry Island was a special treat, but generally speaking children made their own amusements. Only exceptionally would there be more serious casualties than wet clothing or a broken limb.

Christening, 20 March 1929. Mr and Mrs Arthur Davies and their son Cyril, outside the west door of the Cathedral after the baptism of their younger son, Eric.

In the afternoon George Julian and John Andrews were admitted. 41 children were present.

Tuesday. February 11th. In the morning the Revd D Morgan brought James Davis to school. Margaret and Alice Matthews were admitted. I began to teach the children "The Sermon on the Mount". In the afternoon I gave the 3rd class a lesson on "counting". 44 children were present morning & afternoon.

Wednesday. February 12th. In the morning I gave the children a lesson on the "Early life of Abram". In the afternoon Miss Allibant visited the school. 41 children were present in the morning and 42 in the afternoon.

Thursday. February 13th. In the morning I gave the children a lesson on the "Stick" continued from last week. In the afternoon Mrs Simpers and Mrs Meddler visited the school. 44 children were present in the morning and 41 in the afternoon.

Friday. February 14th. In the morning I examined the children in New Testament History. In the afternoon the Revd D Morgan visited school. 43 children present in the morning & 42 afternoon.

Infants School, 1868. This page from the log book of Llandaff (Infants) National School for a week in February 1868 records admissions, attendances, the subjects taught and the visitors who came to observe.

Llandaff National School, 1896 showing the children of the Infants' School, photographed in the playground of the Prichard building. Second from the left in the front row is Charles Wilson David Cox, son of William Cox who was apprenticed to John Prichard.

Group 8 at Llandaff Junior School, *c.* 1900 with Miss Knill(?) the headmistress and Miss Brothwell, the assistant head.

Group 1 at Llandaff National School (Boys), 1912-13. Mr Harper, headmaster and choirmaster is on the right. In the second row from the back and fifth from the left is R.A. Durnell.

Llandaff Infants' School, 1932. From left to right, back row: David Trimm, Margaret Cox, Cyril Davies, Jean McIntyre, John Haskell, Edna Hole, Donald Parry, Nancy Greenslade, -?-. Front row: Roy Morris, Pamela Owen, Ivy Fowler, Trevor May, Marcel Hopkins, Jean Evans.

Sam Rex, deputy conductor of the orchestra, rehearsing for the Cardiff Schools Festival, Llandaff Infants' School, 1935. Sheila Weedon is having her wrist position adjusted.

Form 2 at Llandaff Church in Wales Junior School, 1936. The pupils from left to right, back row : Haydn Beach, Bernard Bradshaw, Thomas Brooks, Leslie Mitchell, Norman Hill, -?-, George Evans. Middle row: -?-, Raymond Spear, Mary Edge, Joyce Hill, Doreen Gould, Sheila Clay, Marion Jenkins, William Gore. Front row: Margaret Trott, Sheila Weedon, -?-, Nancy Greenslade, Edith Bailey, Edna Watts, Lilian Hocking, Pat Hole, Mavis Trimm, Grace Cole. A relief teacher is on the left and Sam Rex, headmaster, is on the right.

Llandaff Church Junior School, High Street, 1867. This building, designed by John Prichard to cater for an expanding school population, stood on the site now occupied by the block of shops adjacent to the Butchers Arms. Both the infants and the junior departments were previously in the premises which are now the Llandaff Institute.

41

Llandaff Infants School, 12 April 1935. From left to right, back row: Mavis Trimm, Sheila Weedon, Edna Hole, Margaret Trott(?), Edith Bailey, Marjorie Jenkins. Front row, extreme left: Eric Davies; extreme right: Fred Pollard.

Llandaff National School, *c.* 1900, pictured in the garden of the headmaster's house, apparently after a cup-winning performance, perhaps at the Cardiff Schools Music Festival. Black Hall and No 4, Heol Fair show through the trees. The post office has, by this date, moved from No 5, Heol-y-Pavin to Imperial Buildings.

Llandaff Church Sunday school in procession up High Street with their banner, preceded by their band. On the right is the wall of the Junior School. Horse-drawn cabs can be seen waiting outside the Maltsters Arms at the bottom of High Street. On the left is the William Evans Bakery - later to be Woods and Seig.

Llandaff Sunday school teachers, c. 1880. The recently appointed Vicar of Llandaff, James Rice Buckley, is in the middle of the back row.

Band of Hope, *c.* 1880. Vicar Buckley, seated centre right, was an ardent supporter of the Temperance Movement, refusing to attend any Parish Council or other meeting which took place on licensed premises.

The Cathedral School, Llandaff, *c.* 1880. An early picture of the Choir School which had been started at No 32, Bridge Street on the initiative of Minor Canon Fishbourne. The school was refounded by Dean Vaughan in 1880, when it moved to Green Court. The headmaster in this photograph is thought to be Charles Butler.

The Cathedral School, *c.* 1890. The pupils are photographed in the front garden of Green Court, their new premises. In the 1891 census the following names of staff appear: 'Headmaster: Revd Ernest Owen, aged 34, born in Birmingham; Assistant Masters: F.L.T. Dent, aged 26, born in Manningtree, Essex and Arthur Spencer, aged 23, from Newcastle upon Tyne.'

The Cathedral School Cricket XI, 1917. From left to right, back row: G. Holland, W.M.A. Jones, R.L.D. Cattley, W.E. Gaccon. Middle row: R. Faulks, D. Holland, R.J. Cameron (Captain), G.L. Jones, P.H.P. Hill. Front: A.R. Wilkinson, T.L. Richards.

The Cathedral School outside the north door of the Cathedral, *c.* 1917. Staff, seated from left to right: Mr Symons(?), Mr G.L. Robathan, Canon David Davies, the Very Revd Charles E.T. Griffith, Mr Rollo Bryce-Smith, Mr Lanion(?), Mr George Beale (Cathedral organist and choirmaster). Robathan and Bryce-Smith later left to start their own school, and Theodore Coombs became headmaster.

The boys of Elm Tree House School, *c.* 1935. Miss D.G. Winslade taught maths and also apparently had a special responsibility for the boys; these are 'Miss Winslade's little boys'. She left teaching for industry during the Second World War and died in 1983. From left to right, back row: David Evans, Roy Barnet, Roger Barltrop, John Lewis, John Evans, Alan Grest, Peter Halewood. Middle row: Willoughby Jones, John Whitehead, Garth Diamond, Michael Lloyd, Billy Cropley. Front row: Charles Saunders, Ken Thomas, John Payn, David Andrews, John Billingham, Tony Mitchell, David Imry.

Elm Tree House hockey team, *c.* 1935.

Howell's School, *c.* 1860. The school was first established in 1860 with the object of providing an education for orphan girls and also for fee paying pupils. Miss Baldwin, the headmistress until 1872, and the first orphans appear in this photograph. Also shown, in the back row second from the left, is Richard Church, gardener, and on the far right, George White, house steward.

Headmistress and boarders at Howell's School, 1890. Miss Maria Kendall, headmistress between 1880 and 1920, was born in Yeovil in 1843, educated at a private school on the Isle of Wight and in Paris, and held various private teaching posts before acquiring qualifications and ultimately being appointed to Llandaff in 1880.

Howell's School hockey team, 1890.

A botany expedition from Howell's School, 1911. The party was led by Miss Winny to Mynydd y glew near Peterston.

The cookery school at Howell's, c. 1930.

Miss M.Ll. Lewis (headmistress of Howell's School, 1941-77). When Margaret Lewis was appointed as headmistress of Howell's School at the age of 31, she was the youngest public school headmistress in the country. After reading English at Oxford and playing lacrosse for Wales, she came well equipped to keep the balance between 'mens' and 'corpus', and with faith and courage enough to carry the huge responsibility of a boarding school in wartime. 'Howell's School IS Miss Lewis', was the view during her 36 years in charge. She died suddenly in October 1980 after a tragically short retirement.

Bishop of Llandaff Church in Wales High School, 1980. John Gould, teacher of art and drama, rehearsing pupils for his production of *Crucified*, a play for Passiontide by John Gould and Peter Wingfield. From left to right: Helen Isaacs, David Lloyd, Marco Fiera, Keith Thomas, John Gould.

David Lloyd as Christ in *Crucified*, 1980. Performed in Llandaff Cathedral, the series of plays devised by John Gould had a profound influence on the generation of Bishop of Llandaff pupils involved in the productions.

51

Llandaff Cathedral Scout Troop, 1916. Third row, seated fifth from the left, is R.A. Durnell. On his left is scoutmaster Harry Cleves and on *his* left, Archdeacon Buckley.

1st Llandaff (Cathedral) Scouts, 1934. Bishop Timothy Rees is seated fourth from the right.

2nd Llandaff Guide Company, *c.* 1919 in the garden of 'Cheverell', the Bassetts' house (now No 19, The Cathedral Green). Seated, second from the left, is Kit Bassett, Guide captain. On her left is her lieutenant, Elsie Wain, sister of Captain R. Wain VC. The colour bearer on the extreme right is Violet Finnimore, one of the first four guides when the company was founded.

1st Llandaff Guide Company, 1954. Marian Everett receives her second class badge from Miss Nancy Fletcher, the County Commissioner. (The boxes on the platform are goods to go to the Llandaff parish stall at the Edward Nicholl Home fête in Penylan). As a brownie in 1952 Marian had contracted polio and spent a year in hospital in Cowbridge. A remarkable example of fortitude and cheerfulness, she flew up to guides in 1953 and gained her second class badge so quickly that, exceptionally, it was presented by the County Commissioner. The calliper on her right leg and 'mousetrap' on her right hand are hardly apparent. Marian went on to first class, became Captain of the company and latterly Training Adviser for Wales. After a full and productive life she is now cheering everyone up at Dan-y-Bryn Cheshire Home, Radyr.

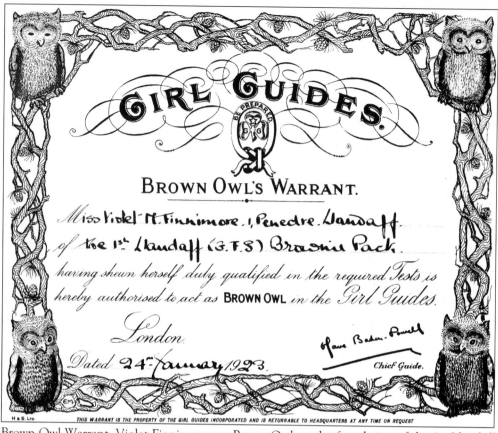

GIRL GUIDES.

BE PREPARED

BROWN OWL'S WARRANT.

Miss Violet M. Finnimore, 1, Penedre. Llandaff
of the 1st Llandaff (G.F.S) Brownie Pack.

having shewn herself duly qualified in the required Tests is
hereby authorised to act as **BROWN OWL** *in the Girl Guides.*

London.

Dated 24th January 1923.

Olave Baden-Powell
Chief Guide.

THIS WARRANT IS THE PROPERTY OF THE GIRL GUIDES INCORPORATED AND IS RETURNABLE TO HEADQUARTERS AT ANY TIME ON REQUEST

Brown Owl Warrant. Violet Finnimore was Brown Owl on the foundation of the 1st Llandaff (GFS) Brownie Pack in 1923. The 1st Llandaff Guides were, at that time, GFS (Girls' Friendly Society).

1st Llandaff Brownies outing to Merthyr Mawr in the 1920s.

Four

Work

Before the Glamorganshire Canal opened in 1794, Llandaff people no doubt followed the trades and occupations common in any rural community of the time. There would have been farmers and market gardeners, innkeepers and carpenters, millers and flannel fullers together with thatchers, blacksmiths and weavers. These trades helped to make the community almost self sufficient.

With the improvement of transport in the first half of the nineteenth century many local producers and craftsmen were, however, superseded by specialist manufacturers such as the brickmakers of the Midlands and the textile mills of the North. Leather goods were now factory-made and grocer's shops opened to sell the wider range of foodstuffs which became available. The canal itself not only generated its own trades such as boat building and repairing, but also resulted in the development along its banks of other industries which relied on the carriage of materials and finished goods by the canal boats. Examples of these were the soap works and the patent fuel works which sprang up on the east bank of the River Taff, and the Evans' Eagle Foundry in Llandaff Yard (Llandaff North) whose cast-iron products can still be seen on the streets of Cardiff. It was here, and at the College Iron Works, that iron from Merthyr Tydfil came to be processed and finished. The building of the Taff Vale and the South Wales Railway (later to become the Great Western Railway) also brought new occupations to Llandaff, and enabled people who worked in Cardiff to live further from the centre than before.

As Llandaff increasingly became a preferred residential area in the latter years of the nineteenth century, so its industry largely disappeared. In place of industry, educational and communications establishments appeared. In addition to the range of primary and secondary schools which one might expect in any community, Llandaff attracted, over the years, a wide variety of educational institutions - private preparatory schools and a public school for girls, the Cathedral Choir School, a technical college which is now part of the Cardiff College of Higher Education, and St Michael's Theological College. For some years a specialist Maritime College (based in Fairwater) and the College of Home Economics occupied sites in Llandaff but both these have ceased to operate here and their premises have been put to other uses.

The advent of commercial television in South Wales in the 1950s saw the opening of a studio centre by Television Wales and the West (TWW), later HTV, around the Georgian farmhouse at Pontcanna, and the short-lived Wales West and North company erected studios and offices behind the old Mill House on Western Avenue which are now used by the Welsh Joint Education Committee. The BBC also moved to Llandaff when its engineering branch came to Baynton House. In 1967 they built a new studio centre on the Baynton House site and moved their sound broadcasting activities there from Park Place, Cardiff. Television services, previously based in Broadway in Roath, followed shortly after. In recent years expansion has taken place across Llantrisant Road into the former College of Home Economics.

The place of the small craftsmen of former years has, at least partially, been taken by the small architectural, financial services and information technology consultancies, whilst the grocers, butchers and similar purveyors of necessities have increasingly lost the competition with out-of-town supermarkets and been replaced by shops catering for the tourist and luxury trades.

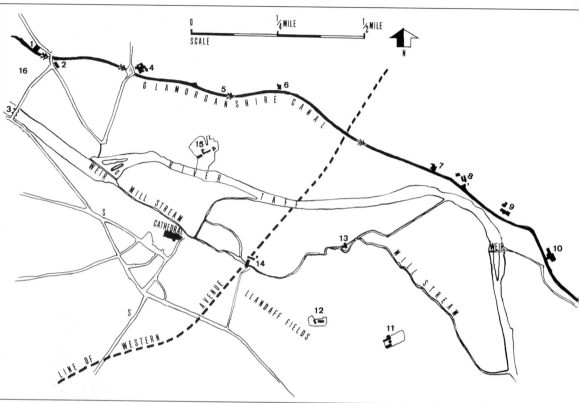

Industry in Llandaff, 1886. 1. Eagle Foundry; 2. Cow & Snuffers; 3. Llandaff Bridge; 4. College Iron Works; 5. Canal Graving Dock; 6. Cambrian Patent Fuel Works; 7. Anchor Patent Fuel Works; 8. Soap Works (disused); 9. Crown Patent Fuel Works; 10. Star Patent Fuel Works; 11. Pontcanna Farm; 12. Court Farm; 13. Tucking Mill; 14. Corn Mill; 15. Gabalva House; 16. Crown Match Factory: S. Smithy.

Drain cover, outside Llandaff Cathedral's west door, which was manufactured at the Eagle Foundry, c. 1870.

The flotchet, 1893. The water for
the Mill Stream was taken from the
River Taff above Llandaff Weir, its
volume being controlled by means of
a sluice gate, or, in the local
vernacular, a flotchet.

The Mill Stream. This water-course flowed eastward from the flotchet alongside a footpath below Dean's Wood. The path remains but the Mill Stream is now no more than a shallow depression.

The Mill Stream. The first crossing of the Mill Stream was near the Prebendal House, where a small metal footbridge gave access to the Arls Field.

The Mill Stream, *c*. 1880. The second crossing of the Mill Stream was made by a handsome stone bridge, designed by John Prichard. It connected the grandly named 'Transpontine' churchyard (opened in 1860) with the north churchyard which was first used for burial in March 1883.

Llandaff Mill and Mill Pond. Essential to the operation of a water-mill was an adequate reservoir of water. The Mill Pond which satisfied this need for the Llandaff Corn Mill was situated on the ground now occupied by the Llandaff RFC clubhouse and the waste ground behind it, adjacent to the footpath to the Cathedral.

East side of Llandaff Mill. This fine, four-storied corn mill was demolished in the mid-1930s to make way for the construction of Western Avenue. All that remains today is a low arched channel, crossing beneath Western Avenue, at the junction between Llandaff Rugby Club and the College grounds. Mill House, built in the Victorian period for the miller, is now a part of the Welsh Joint Education Committee (WJEC) office complex. After driving the corn mill the water flowed on to power the 'tucking' (or fulling) mill, the buildings of which are adjacent to the Cardiff Equestrian Centre, before returning to the river some distance below Blackweir.

The Toll-gate. On Saturday, 7 June 1788, the County Road Commissioners had their attention drawn to the popular practice of fording the River Taff at Llandaff thereby avoiding payment at the Toll-gate. The Commissioners steepened the river banks at the point where the old road forded the Taff (to College Road) so as to compel the use of the bridge and the payment of the toll. The road leading to the left, now Llantrisant Road, was at one time known as Pentyrch Street.

Cow and Snuffers and Llandaff Lock. The public house on this site was originally called the Red Cow, but the present name derives from the time of an Irish servant of Sir Robert Lynch Blosse, Bt, of Gabalva, and has been the source of considerable speculation. It is now generally accepted that it arose from the lyric of a song in a musical farce first printed in Dublin in 1801. Llandaff Lock, No 45 in the length of the Glamorganshire Canal - which opened in 1794 - is one of four locks within the old parish of Llandaff. It was immediately upstream of the narrow hump-backed road bridge at the junction of Bridge Road with Station Road in Llandaff Yard (Llandaff North).

Eagle Foundry, Llandaff Yard, September 1890. This foundry on the bank of the canal immediately adjacent to Llandaff Lock, received its raw material by barge from the iron works of Merthyr Tydfil. Man-hole and drain covers, street signs and direction posts bearing the legend 'Evans, Llandaff' can still be seen in profusion in and around Cardiff, bearing witness to the output of this small foundry.

Miss Bessie Evans, the daughter of the owner of the Eagle Foundry seen in a pony and trap in September 1890. The identity of the driver is unknown.

Telephone operators, Llandaff, 1912. The telephone exchange in Llandaff at this time was at No 14, Heol Fair. Ethel Sone, at the extreme left, and her sister Elizabeth, at the right in the back row, worked at the exchange.

The kitchen at the Bishop's Palace, 10 October 1916. Margaret Button, the housekeeper, is on the right.

Convalescence, 1916. Both 'The Lodge', in Cardiff Road, and St Michael's Theological College were pressed into use during the First World War as convalescent homes for wounded servicemen. Seen on the steps of 'The Lodge', with a group of convalescents, are some of nursing staff who cared for them. At the right in the second row stands Margaret Button (see opposite page).

VAD nurse, 1916. Lilian May Osborne nursed both at St Michael's College and at 'The Lodge'. She appears on the right of the back row in the group photograph. Trained as a teacher, she later became headmistress of North Church Street School in the Docks, and died in 1979 in the Hendre Nursing Home at the age of 91.

Llandaff Technical College, 1952. One of the largest building projects in the area in the years immediately following the Second World War was the construction of a new technical college on a 'green field' site off Western Avenue. The contract, in the sum of £184,895, was placed with Messrs McLaughlin and Harvey for completion in twenty-one months. Site work started in September 1952.

Llandaff Technical College, 1953. The reinforced concrete barrel-vaulted roof spanned the various workshop areas, giving large uninterrupted space for machine tools and for vehicle maintenance courses. The trees in the background line Western Avenue.

Llandaff Technical College, March 1953. The truncated spire of the Cathedral, as yet unrestored, is visible through the steel skeleton of the main block which faces Western Avenue.

Llandaff Technical College, autumn 1954. The contract was completed within the specified time and the college welcomed its first students on 20 September 1954. The official opening was carried out by HRH The Duke of Edinburgh on Wednesday 1 December 1954.

The Strawberry Fields, 1892. The area around Llandaff enjoyed a long and noted reputation as a centre of market gardening. Records confirm that vegetables from Llandaff were sold on the quay at Bristol in the eighteenth century, perhaps provisioning ships engaged in the transatlantic slave and sugar trades. The Strawberry Fields might well be part of this market gardening industry and occupied the ground which is now the site of the Llandaff Rowing Club.

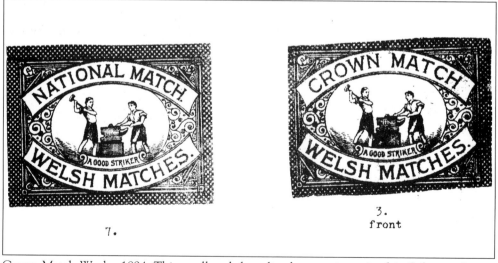

Crown Match Works, 1894. This small and short-lived enterprise existed in Solomon Street, Llandaff Yard between 1894 and 1898 when the works went into voluntary liquidation.

Five

Play

'The great holiday of the year,' reported Vicar Buckley, 'was Whitsun, when the Llandaff Pleasure Fair was held. Every cottage was transformed into a 'Bush House', so called because a green bush was hung at the entrance to indicate that beer was sold there, and many cottages relied on the takings to pay their rent for the whole year.' One little girl from Chapel Street used to run into the house when she heard the drums, because she was afraid of the dancing bear. Another, too young to go to the fair with her sister, looked out of the window of The Cottage and remembered that there was a fat lady and a calf with two heads. It was 1880, and that was the last Whit Fair, after 674 years.

One of the earliest and most popular ball games in Llandaff was a form of fives. This was played by teams of four or five men against the wall of the Malt House adjoining the Maltsters Arms 'with half the adult male population looking on.' There was another ball court attached to the Heathcock Hotel, and even the north wall of the Cathedral was pressed into use, much to the distress of the bishop. 'To be a crack ball player in those days,' remembered Ebenezer Moses in the 1880s, 'made a man a hero.'

The Llandaff Debating Society flourished in the early 1900s, meeting in the Maltsters Arms, 'a very select drinking club' compared with the Working Men's Club (now The Institute).

The River Taff was always a fascinating place. However, it had lost its charm for bathers since the effluent from the collieries upstream gave a noticeable taint to both air and water. Since the pits have closed, however, the water has gradually regained transparency, and wildlife of all sorts is returning. Salmon and sewin can once more be seen leaping the weirs as in former days.

Gardening was, of course, a livelihood for much of Llandaff's history, but it was also a productive recreation, especially during the two world wars. Allotments survived in the Arls Field and along Pwllmelin and Radyr Court Road for many years, but have now been extinguished by residential and educational development. There are, however, still allotments in Pontcanna Fields.

The increasing leisure time in the years which followed the Second World War provided fertile ground for the growth of musical and dramatic activity. The Cathedral Special Choir, renamed the Llandaff Cathedral Choral Society, and the operatic and dramatic societies still survive, although there is no longer a hall suitable for dramatic performances other than in the schools.

Llandaff is surrounded by parks. Llandaff Fields have long been the place for football, baseball, hockey and cricket, and the generosity of the Thompson family secured them with a covenant so far impregnable and guarded by 'Park Watch'. The conversion of Charles Thompson's garden into Thompson's Park in 1891 and of Llandaff Common into Victoria Park in 1897 enriched the southern approach, Hailey Park lies to the north and St Fagans is not far to the west. Since the gift to the City of Cardiff of Cardiff Castle and Bute Park by the Marquess of Bute in 1947 it has been possible to walk on either side of the Taff from Llandaff to Cardiff, or - better still - from Cardiff to Llandaff!

Tennis party at the Bishop's Palace, *c.* 1882. The elderly lady in black is thought to be Mrs Georgina Lewis, the Bishop's wife.

Taff Rowing Club, Llandaff, 1886. Photographed outside Riversdale House, Radyr Court Road after a victorious season which included winning the four-oared outrigged race at Penarth on 28 July and the City Challenge Cup at Llandaff on 1 September 1886 (value 20 guineas). The Llandaff crew is from left to right: J. Smith (stroke), A. Smith (No 3), J. Lovering (No 2), F. Lovering (bow). In front is F. Matthews (cox).

Taff Rowing Club coxed four pulling away from the club, early 1900s. The stroke was Alfred Edwin Osborne who was killed in Jerusalem during the First World War.

Llandaff Regatta, c. 1930. The Cardiff Rowing Club boathouse is visible behind the flags. This photograph was apparently taken from the island on which the band was usually accommodated, and pre-dates the foundation of the Llandaff Rowing Club in 1946.

Llandaff Football Club (sic), 1891-92. Formed in 1876, the Llandaff Rugby Football Club reputedly took its colours of Oxford and Cambridge blue after two early captains from those universities. One of the earliest clubs in the Welsh Rugby Union, Llandaff won the South Wales Challenge Cup during the 1891-92 season. From left to right: T. Gibbons (Hon. Secretary), A.T. Thomas, L. Howe, T. Davies, W. Millward, I. Brain, T. Goodfellow, D.B. Radley, E. Phillips (Umpire). Seated: J. Glendening, J. Elliot (Captain), H.E. Harris (Vice-Captain), W. Harding. Front row: J. Davies, W. Davies, H. Marks, D. Llewellyn.

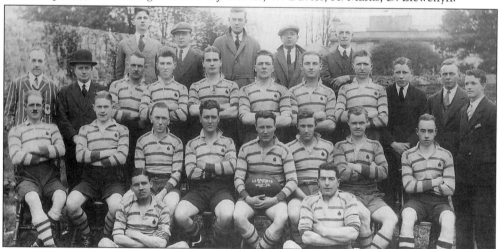

Llandaff Rugby Football Club, 1925-26 season. Llandaff has always played on the Bishop's Field, though its dressing room accommodation has progressed from making use of local pubs, converting the Bishop's old farm building on the field and later adding the old Llandavian Cricket Pavilion as refreshment and committee rooms. In the early 1960s these buildings had to be demolished in the interests of scenic beauty and for a season or so the club camped out in the Pound (alongside the castle). In 1963 the site of the present clubhouse was acquired. This group is outside the castle wall in Court Lane, with the Bishop's Palace in the background. From left to right, second row from back: E.L. Ford (Hon. Treasurer), D.C. Hopkins (Chairman), A. Thomas, A. James, H. Johnson, P. Cravos, T. Gadd, E. Griffiths, V.R. Osmond, D.H. Weaver, J.H. Thomas (Vice Chairman) Seated: B. Bolt, J.D. Bell, W. Richards (Hon. Secretary), W.R. James (Vice-Captain), A.E. James (Captain), R. Berry, H. Birch, J. Weston. Front: L. Sloman, W. Samuels.

Swimming baths, Llandaff Fields, 1929. A well used amenity for many years, the baths have recently been closed and the area filled with rubble from the demolished Court Farm. The buildings in the background are Llandaff Corn Mill on the left and Mill House to the right.

Insole Fields, near the present Insole Place, showing a Victoria Park Sunday school treat, with Mr W.H. Tanner in charge, 1931. In the background: the rise towards Fairwater Road, the cinder path railings behind the trees and, on the far left, the beginning of work on Western Avenue which has been temporarily halted.

The Maltsters Arms, 1939. Structurally, it has hardly changed since the days when the Llandaff Debating Society met here. Members included the chairman, Charlie Hopkins; Tom Evans of the bakery; Albert Bolt of Bolt's Stores on The Green; and Mr Asplin, greengrocer, whose shop was next door. The Debating Society was known as 'a very select drinking club' in contrast to the Working Men's Club (now the Llandaff Institute) and flourished *c.* 1910. Points of interest are the telephone number (Llandaff 61), the sign showing that Ely Road was at that time a one way street and the poster for the Prince of Wales Theatre where *Worth a Million* starred Edmund Gwenn and Claude Hulbert. The Sunday concert by Richard Tauber would probably have been in held in the Park Hall Cinema, as there was no other suitable concert hall at that time.

Bonfire night, in the lane behind Palace Avenue, mid-1930s. From left to right: Philip Chorley, Douglas Weedon, Peter Boswell, David Morgan, George Evans, Sheila Weedon, Nancy Greenslade, -?-, Jean Boswell.

Mothers' Union outing to Weston-super-Mare, 28 June 1938. This trip was by Campbell's steamer, of course, and it was a rough crossing! In the coach, second window from the left: Mrs Frewer and Mrs Wadsworth. Third window: Canon D. Akrill Jones, Vicar. In the doorway: Mrs Pollard and Mrs Hill. Among those standing, from the right: Mrs Weedon, Eva Coles, Doris Cox, Gwen Trimm, and Mrs Sloper.

The Parish fête, on the Cathedral School Field, c. 1938. In the back row, third from the right: Mrs Weedon. Seated, third from the right: Mrs Jenkins, Pontcanna. Seated on the ground: Mrs Harris. 'There'll always be a Llandaff, while there's a Parish fête, with Mr Charlie Morgan selling programmes at the gate.'

VE Day party on The Green, 8 May 1945, with the Cathedral School in the background.

VJ Day party in Heol-y-Pavin, 15 August 1945. Standing, from left to right: Mr Ben Songhurst from London and Mollie Winston (whom he later married); Mr Green (holding baby); Mrs Green (No 4, Penedre); Mrs Werrett (No 2, Penedre); Mrs Broderick (No 3, Penedre); Miss Finnimore (No 1, Penedre); Margaret Ferris ; Mollie Ferris (No 11), with her parents just visible behind her; Mrs Samuel (No 1); Mr Green (No 4, Penedre); Tom Gasson (No 7); Walter Hailes (No 5); Mr Griffiths (No 9); Lewis Samuel (No 1); Fred Winston (No 11). Middle row, partly hidden: Stuart and Stanley Green (No 4, Penedre), Brian Griffiths (No 9), David Samuel (No 1). Front row: Mrs Griffiths (No 9); Mollie and Brian Griffiths; Sylvia Horne (No 3); Ronald Horne (No 3); Mrs Horne (No 3); Margaret Samuel (with dog); Lucy Green (No 5); Mrs Hailes (No 5); Elsie Jenkins; Ada Gasson. All house numbers are for Heol-y-Pavin unless otherwise indicated.

Llandaff Citizens' Association pageants. The contribution of the Citizens' Association to the Festival of Britain was a pageant of life in the Cathedral City from the Bronze Age to the present time, entitled *The Llandaff Story*. It was performed at Insole Court from 6 to 8 September 1951 by a cast of over one hundred members of the association directed by the author, Mrs F. Louise Hanson. Two years later, there was another pageant at Insole Court to celebrate the coronation of Elizabeth II. Called *The Three Queens*, it dealt with the reigns of Elizabeth I, Queen Anne and Queen Victoria. In the photograph below are a few of the cast. The group includes: Harry Thorne, W. Edward Phillips, Alderman George E.B. Frewer, Miss Jessica Frewer, Martha Lawday, Walter Williams, Bernard Cross, Mrs Dorothy Cox.

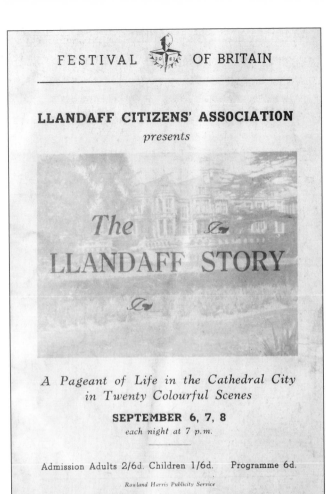

FESTIVAL OF BRITAIN

LLANDAFF CITIZENS' ASSOCIATION

presents

The LLANDAFF STORY

A Pageant of Life in the Cathedral City in Twenty Colourful Scenes

SEPTEMBER 6, 7, 8

each night at 7 p.m.

Admission Adults 2/6d. Children 1/6d.   Programme 6d.

Rowland Harris Publicity Service

Everyman at Llandaff Cathedral in 1947. This was produced in the ruined Cathedral by Mary David, and played against the west door and gallery. From left to right: Marcel Hopkins, Muriel Sparkes, Maureen Gould, John Lewis, Peggy Scard, Dorette Gould, Jack Payn. Bishop John Morgan, out of sight in the tower, was the voice of God.

Jack Payn and Dorette Gould in duet during the Cymry'r Groes pantomime - *A Tale of True Love*, July 1949. This was the last of a series of 'summer pantomimes', written by Maureen Butcher (née Gould) with music by Vernon Butcher for performance at the Parish fête.

Six

The Cathedral

Tradition has it that there has been a place of Christian worship at Llandaff since the year AD 560. The early building would have been small, and the discovery of a number of early British graves at the western end of the nave in 1884 would add credence to the supposed antiquity of the site. The first building of which any substantial evidence remains is that erected by Urban, Bishop of Llandaff between 1107 and 1133. This church was probably cruciform with an apsidal east end and was about 150 feet in length. Of this building, the most notable features which survive are the semi-circular decorated arch at the high altar, two vestigial arches in the south wall of the sanctuary, and the north and south doorways which appear to have been moved to their present positions during subsequent phases of the Cathedral's expansion.

During the Early English period the building grew westward to its present length, terminating with the west front, much of which dates from c. 1220. The central section of the west front was flanked by a pair of towers, both of which have been replaced in later centuries. Building continued and with the construction of the Lady - or 'Welsh' - Chapel c. 1280, the church had reached approximately its present dimensions. Further work and embellishment continued until the middle years of the fourteenth century.

The damage caused by Owain Glyn Dŵr in the first decade of the fifteenth century, coupled with the increasing lawlessness of the time, ushered in a bleak period of the Cathedral's history which was relieved only by some restoration in the latter half of that century, which included the construction of the north-west (Jasper) bell-tower.

The Reformation (1529-1559) resulted in the impoverishment of both the Cathedral and the diocese, reducing the number of resident clergy and stripping the building of many of its treasures. Only eighty years later, the Civil War and the Commonwealth brought about the closure of much of the Cathedral and the secular use of most of the building. Only the Lady Chapel survived as a place of worship. By the end of the seventeenth century choral services had been abandoned even in the Lady Chapel and the whole building had begun to fall into ruin. Storms during the first quarter of the eighteenth century contributed to the collapse of the south-west tower and much of the nave roof. Between 1730 and 1752 an attempt at restoration in the classical style to the designs of John Wood the Elder was made but never completed.

With the growth of industrialisation in South Wales during the early years of the nineteenth century, coupled with religious revival and the re-institution of the office of dean, serious attempts at restoration began in 1840, and by 1869 a total restoration, including the building of the south-west tower and spire, had been completed. The architects were John Prichard, whose father Richard was one of the Cathedral clergy, and John P. Seddon, who was influential in bringing in members of the Pre-Raphaelite Brotherhood to enhance the work.

In 1941, however, disaster struck once more when a German land-mine exploded in the south churchyard on the evening of 2 January. The roofs of the nave, south aisle and chapter house were almost totally destroyed and much of the Victorian furniture and decorative work was lost. The eastern end of the Cathedral was temporarily repaired and used for worship between April 1942 and April 1957, when restoration under the direction of George Pace was largely completed. This restoration included substantial additions which encompassed the concrete pulpitum carrying the figure of Christ in Majesty (by Sir Jacob Epstein), the Welch Regiment Memorial Chapel on the north side and a range of vestries and offices. On 6 August 1960 the conclusion of this latest major restoration was signalled by a service of thanksgiving held in the presence of HM The Queen and HRH The Duke of Edinburgh.

View from the south-west, 1846, showing the west front of John Wood's Italianate Temple standing amongst the ruins of the Gothic Cathedral. One bay of the medieval clerestory escaped destruction and from this fragment John Prichard, in his nineteenth century restoration, was able to reconstruct the upper nave walls to their original form. The upper room of the chapter house, on the right, housed the village school.

Interior of the nave, 1816. A series of engravings by J. Storer, of which this is one, gave an accurate picture of the ruinous state into which the Cathedral had fallen.

John Prichard, architect (1817-1886). He was the only son of the Senior Vicar Choral of the Cathedral, and trained in the London office of Walker, the chief assistant to A.W.N. Pugin. Prichard was responsible, in partnership with John Seddon, for the total restoration of the Cathedral. He was also responsible for several other buildings in Llandaff and for many new (and restored) churches, schools and parsonage houses across South Wales.

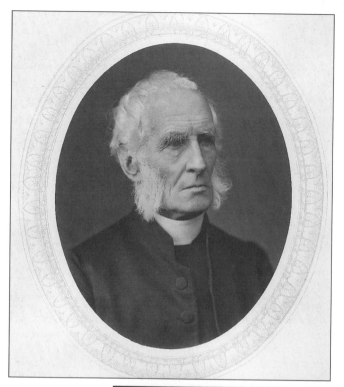

Alfred Ollivant, (Bishop of Llandaff 1849-1882). The first Bishop in several centuries to take up permanent residence in the Diocese, Bishop Ollivant gave enormous encouragement and assistance to those who were restoring the Cathedral and was responsible for a vast programme of church building throughout the diocese as population burgeoned with industrialisation.

William Daniel Conybeare (Dean 1846-1857). The restoration, which had started under Dean Bruce Knight, was continued during its crucial years under the direction of Dean Conybeare, who already had an international reputation as a geologist. He was regarded as a particular expert on the geology of the South Wales coalfield.

View from the east, *c*. 1855. The construction of the tracery of the east window of the Lady Chapel was the first item of restoration undertaken by Prichard. By the time that a photographic record commenced much of the restoration of the eastern end of the Cathedral was complete, but as can be seen, the crown of the north-west tower, the upper floor of the chapter house and the whole of the south-west tower had yet to be tackled.

South side of the Cathedral, 1866. Construction work on the parapet of the south aisle had yet to be completed, and the row of sovereigns' heads, so much a feature of the south wall, was, at this stage, still a row of uncarved blocks. Work on the south-west tower and the crown of the north-west tower had not yet started but the newly erected monument to Dean Conybeare stood near the chapter house.

View from the east, *c.* 1880. Looking across his garden, now the site of 'Clock House', Mr Clement Waldron, who lived in 'White House' on The Green, would have seen the completed Cathedral.

View from the Arls Field, *c.* 1890. The Prebendal House, with its first floor bay window, has since been extended both towards the Mill Stream in the 1920s and towards the Cathedral in the post-Second World War restoration. The tree at the extreme right, a cut-leafed beech (*Fagus Sylvatica Laciniata*), was felled in 1995.

Interior of the Cathedral, looking east, pre-1900. Features which marked the Victorian restoration were the high chancel arch, subsequently lowered to allow for the re-introduction of a flat panelled ceiling, the triptych reredos by Dante Gabriel Rossetti, and the heavy wooden pews and choir stalls. The organ, by Gray and Davison, was installed in 1861, but was replaced by a new and larger instrument in 1900. The old organ with its unusual forward facing trumpet pipes is still in use in Usk parish church.

Llandaff Cathedral choir, c. 1870. Before the foundation of the Cathedral Choir School, services were led by a local voluntary choir. Among the choirboys seated on the steps of the Conybeare memorial is William Goscombe John, later to become Sir William, the famous sculptor. His father, Thomas John, sang bass in the same choir and is seated on the top step of the memorial.

The font. Placed under the second arch of the south arcade, the spot occupied by the present font, this font was presented to the Cathedral in 1863 by Dean Thomas Williams. Dean Williams had succeeded Dean Conybeare in 1857 and had carried forward the restoration to its conclusion. The panels of the font represented subjects from the story of the Flood.

The pulpit. Designed by Prichard and Seddon and executed in Caen stone, this pulpit stood one bay further east than the present pulpit. The panels, four in number, were modelled by the Pre-Raphaelite sculptor, Thomas Woolner. On one side were the figures of St John and St Paul and on the other, Moses and David. The 'Moses' panel was salvaged from the war-damaged pulpit, as was the head from the 'St John' panel.

Charles John Vaughan (Dean 1879-1897).
Formerly Headmaster of Harrow and at one
time Master of the Temple Church in
London, Dean Vaughan is remembered in
Llandaff for having founded the Cathedral
Choir School in 1880 and for his
contribution to the training of candidates
to the ministry.

Revd J.R.Buckley, (Vicar of Llandaff)

James Rice Buckley (1849-1924).
Throughout Dean Vaughan's time at the
Deanery, the parish of Llandaff had J.R.
Buckley as its vicar. He had come to Llandaff
in 1878 and served the parish until his death
in 1924. For the last ten years of his life he
was also Archdeacon of Llandaff. As
Chairman of the Parish Council he was as
diligent in pursuing the improvement of
living conditions as he was in his spiritual
capacity.

Funeral of William Clarke in 1923. Archdeacon Buckley headed the cortège for the funeral of William Clarke, one of numerous members of the Clarke family who had worked on the Cathedral since the early days of the nineteenth century restoration. Among the mourners were William Goscombe John and William Clarke's two sons, Wyndham and Guy. Guy so loved flowers that he could not bear to cut them, so that the coffin is surmounted by pot plants. When this photograph is compared with that on page 81a one can readily appreciate the changes which had been made in sixty years.

Interior looking east, *c.* 1930. Between 1858 and 1864, Rossetti, one of the leading figures of the Pre-Raphaelite Brotherhood, painted the triptych for the high altar reredos using many of his circle of friends as models. The stonework of the reredos was designed by Prichard and Seddon. The paintings were removed to a place of safety some months prior to the bombing in 1941, but the stonework and the altar steps were removed to allow the formation of an 'Emergency Cathedral' and were not replaced. The new and larger organ had, at the top of its case, six large figures of angels playing various musical instruments. These, together with many of the other smaller box-wood figures which filled the niches on the stalls, were salvaged in 1941 and later gilded and used around the concrete pulpitum in 1957. Much of the woodwork in the Cathedral came from the workshops of William Clarke in Cardiff Road. Some of the figures were the work of Milo ap Griffith, later to become a Royal Academician.

After the bombing, 1941. The land-mine which again reduced the Cathedral to a shell exploded some thirty feet outside the south wall of the building. The nave roof was so extensively damaged that it had to be demolished. The south aisle and Chapter House roofs collapsed and the stone tracery of the windows in the south wall was shattered. The slope of the land south seems to have sheltered the village of Llandaff from the worst effects of the blast.

Interior looking east, summer 1941. The task of demolishing the remains of the nave roof was an extremely hazardous operation, but by the summer of 1941 this had been done and the majority of the shattered furniture had been removed, leaving the roofless nave looking like a builders' yard.

Debris covering the choir stalls and lectern, January 1941. The timber which fell into the nave from the damaged roofs, together with the effects of blast, caused very grave damage to the stalls and pews, most of which were beyond repair, so that the superb Victorian woodcarving was largely lost.

The 'Emergency Cathedral'. On 20 April 1942, that part of the building which lay east of the chancel arch was sufficiently repaired to allow services to resume in what was termed the 'Emergency Cathedral'. The former presbytery served as the nave with the choir and some of the congregation accommodated in the Lady Chapel. Services were accompanied by a Moustel organ, later to be replaced by the pipe organ which now serves in St Luke's Church, Canton.

The Cathedral and Green, 1948. Apart from the portion east of the chancel arch, the Cathedral remained roofless until the early 1950s. The truncated spire was a familiar landmark until the upper third was restored in 1955, the cockerel weather-vane being replaced on 28 July by Dean Eryl Thomas.

Courses of stone from the spire, 1955. Immediately following the bomb damage the top third of the spire, which had shifted, was dismantled and the stone blocks stored. Prior to re-erection, the individual courses of numbered stones were laid out and checked on the floor of the nave.

Reconstruction of the nave and chapter house roofs, 1952. The construction of a new roof continued westward after the lowering of the chancel arch in 1950. Work on the chapter house roof continued simultaneously. At this time the Cathedral School field was still separated from the Bishop's Field by an area of allotments. Further allotments still occupied the area of ground in Llandaff Fields now used for golf.

Rehallowing, 10 April 1957. George G. Pace (left) was appointed architect to the Cathedral in 1949 following the sudden death of Sir Charles Nicholson, who had already commenced the work of restoration. Like Prichard before him, Pace's work appears in many ecclesiastical buildings across South Wales. Sir Jacob Epstein, who came to the west door with Mr Pace that day, had been commissioned by the Dean and Chapter in 1953 to provide a figure of Christ in Majesty for the west face of the new pulpitum.

Rehallowing, 10 April 1957. As almost one of the last acts of his life, Archbishop John Morgan rehallowed, with great solemnity, the restored nave of his Cathedral. The Archbishop was accompanied here by the Cathedral Crucifer, Fred E. Pollard, and four servers, Christopher Harris, Graham Hardy, James Cook and Philip Attwell.

Service of Praise and Thanksgiving, 6 August 1960. Led by the Head Verger, Mr R.T. White, and Dean Eryl Thomas, HM The Queen and HRH The Duke of Edinburgh, with their entourage, leave the Cathedral at the conclusion of the Service of Praise and Thanksgiving to mark the completion of the restoration.

Festival of Music and Drama, 1963. As part of the revitalised life of the Cathedral, a series of annual music festivals was instituted in 1958 on the occasion of the silver jubilee of the Friends of Llandaff Cathedral. An outstanding production which took place in June 1963 was the story of St Teilo in mime, words and music. The score was by William Matthias and the words were by the Venerable J. Gwynno James, Archdeacon of Llandaff. The narrator was John Westbrook, soloists were Helen Watts and Kenneth Bowen, and the choreographer was Geraldine Stephenson.

Seven

Other Notable Buildings

No living community can exist without changing. As the humble wooden church in St Teilo's 'llan' was succeeded by the 'little minster' of stone, and that in turn by Bishop Urban's splendid building of which some features remain, so the scene outside has altered with the passage of time. The old parish boundary included not only Llandaff Yard (now Llandaff North), but Fairwater and part of Pontcanna, and though these have since gained their independence Prichard's spire stands as a reference point and a reminder of the Cathedral's presence from almost every direction.

Dominant as the Cathedral has been, however, even when there were three or four other places of worship in Llandaff, it has not had a monopoly of influence, either architectural or intellectual. The surge of prosperity through the South Wales coalfield towards the end of the nineteenth century enabled benign individuals not only to rebuild the Cathedral but to develop, endow or bequeath other handsome establishments which had their place in the scene. Some buildings have gone without trace, like Green Court, the Vicarage, Baynton House, 'Yscallog' and Fairwater House. The south lodge of Insole Court has disappeared, but the north lodge has been rescued from decay and gentrified. The neat Georgian lodge of Llandaff Court, picturesque but unplumbed, was demolished to make way for the widening of Cardiff Road in 1976. Jonas Watson's 'The Lodge', next door, was spared, and finds a new use as School House for the Cathedral School. Notice the handsome gateposts of No 155, Pencisely Road, which mark what was formerly the entrance to Pencisely House, demolished between the wars. Detective work in Fairwater Road will reveal part of the red brick wall between the Grange and Hardwicke Court built in 'rat-trap' bond cavity construction, for this is where the Morgans of 'Brynderwen' had their peach wall. In counting the losses, including many small cottages, we can be glad that some of the interesting houses of the Victorian age of expansion have been saved and are in useful occupation. Insole Court, Rookwood Hospital and St Michael's College are among the major buildings which deserve, and repay, further study.

Pickard's, c. 1981. This much loved paper and sweet shop and café, which was built c. 1863 for Seaborn the butcher (with a slaughter house next door), closed with the retirement of the founder's second son, Den Pickard, in 1982. In the doorway is Den Pickard with Susie Pengelley, caretaker at the junior school for unnumbered years, as was her mother before her. She retired in 1967 when the old school was due to be demolished.

The last load of hay from Pencisely Field, behind Pencisely House, *c.* 1934. Ben Chandler is on the left, with dogs.

Pencisely Farm, 1930s. The houses of Pencisely Road show through the trees on the right; Pencisely House is hidden by trees towards the left. It was demolished in 1934, and the Pencisely Crescent area was subsequently developed.

'Yscallog', Ely Road, 1930s. This was one of two houses narrowly avoided by the Western Avenue development but then demolished after the Second World War. Rowan Court now occupies all of this site.

The Vicarage, Fairwater Road, early 1960s. Built in the latter years of the nineteenth century, this house was occupied by the vicars of Llandaff until the retirement of Canon Akrill Jones in June 1941. It was then used by the American forces until it returned to use as a clergy house between June 1946 and January 1951. After a period in private occupation, the site was sold for the development known now as The Grange.

Llandaff House, Fairwater Road, 1980s. The original house was owned by Thomas Roberts who died in 1741. His widow married Thomas Edwards, lawyer, Steward to Cardiff Castle, agent to Lady Windsor, and Clerk of the Peace for the County of Glamorgan from 1766 until his death in 1794. Edwards owned property in Manhattan, as well as extensive land holdings throughout Glamorgan, and he rebuilt and extended the house which came as his bride's dowry. Jeremiah Homfray and his son John, both of whom held the office of High Sheriff, lived there. From 1847 to 1860 the building served as the Deanery. By 1871 it was occupied by William Luard, solicitor, landowner and Treasurer of the old County of Glamorgan. A portion of the land had been sold to Edward Stock Hill for the building of 'Rookwood'. In 1900 the property was in the hands of the Gunn family, who divided it into two. Only recently has it been restored to visible unity and the front entrance is now back in its original position.

Ty Gwyn, Fairwater Road, 1950s. Built for Roald Dahl's father in 1907, the house was owned by the Charles Edwards family when it was badly damaged by a parachute mine. This landed at the top of Prospect Drive during the air raid of 2 January 1941 which destroyed the Cathedral. The mine fortunately failed to explode on impact and was detonated on 4 January. The house was commandeered by the army and later used as a NAAFI hostel. Mr and Mrs Edwards are seen standing outside the house to which they had been unable to return until November 1945.

Fairwater House, Fairwater Road in 1994. A rare example of the work of the Glamorgan architect David Vaughan, who also built Miskin Manor (1864), Fairwater House, built *c.* 1840, was for many years the home of the Evan David family. Although a listed building, after passing into the care of the County Council the house was allowed to deteriorate and in 1994 it was demolished.

Two views of Baynton House, 1930s. Built in 1866-8 for Alexander Bassett, by the architect I. Wallis, 'on a field to the left of the Merthyr Road', Baynton House and its eleven-acre site was bought by the BBC after the Second World War and eventually demolished. The site is now occupied by Broadcasting House.

Baynton House lodge, Bridge Road, 1980s. Having survived the demolition of Baynton House in 1975, this little lodge fell into disuse and was finally demolished in the early 1990s.

Mr Evan Lewis's groom brings the horses to the door of 'Brynderwen', Fairwater Road, 1890s.

The gateway to 'Brynderwen', Fairwater Road, c. 1946. This house was built by John Prichard for Mr Evan Lewis, a colliery proprietor. He had a large family and lived there for about forty years. Then John Llewellyn Morgan, son of David Morgan the founder of the Cardiff department store, brought his family here from 'Bryn Teilo' in Llandaff Place about 1907. After the Second World War Colonel H.C. David, of the Evan David family, lived there until his death in 1984. The house was subsequently demolished.

The garden front of 'Brynderwen', c. 1946. The four acres of garden and a tennis court, as well as the site of the house itself, now lie under Hardwicke Court. Attempts to retain the name of 'Brynderwen' for the new development were rebuffed.

The dining room at 'Brynderwen', *c.* 1946.

'Brynderwen', 12 May 1937. John Llewellyn Morgan and his wife Sarah, with their second son Aubrey and youngest son Gerald, plant a beech tree to commemorate the coronation of King George VI. The gardeners are Mr William Edge and Mr Harold Green.

Ely Court, later Insole Court, *c.* 1902. Built in 1855 at a cost of £1,950 for James Harvey Insole, son of George Insole a shipping and colliery proprietor, the house was enlarged and altered many times, as the family's fortune grew. By 1932, however, the routing of the 'orbital road' across the Insole estate occasioned the family to sell what remained to Cardiff City Council for development. At the time of this photograph the porte-cochère (an entrance admitting a carriage) had not been built and the tower still carried the tall roof which was later removed. Note also the curious ventilator on the conservatory.

James Harvey Insole JP (1821-1901). Born in Worcester, James Insole came to Cardiff in 1828 with his father, George Insole, with whom he went into partnership in the colliery and shipowning business in 1842. He was a director of the Penarth Dock and Railway Company and of the Ely Valley Railway.

Arthur Davies with the five cars of the Insole fleet, including two Rolls Royces and a Bentley tourer, for which he was responsible, Insole Court, 1920s.

Mr and Mrs Arthur Davies and their son Cyril, Insole Court north lodge, Fairwater Road, 1926.

Insole Court, December 1944. During the Second World War Insole Court was used by the Auxiliary Fire Service and was also the headquarters of the Cardiff Civil Defence Service, Wardens' Organisation, Western Division. Mr Browning, Divisional Warden, is seen in the middle of the front row.

Insole Court, 1953. In 1949 Alderman George Frewer founded the Llandaff Citizens' Association and ensured that the house was retained for community use. Serious deterioration of the fabric was, however, allowed to spread until recent recognition of the quality of the building and pressure by the Insole Court Action Group (now The Friends of Insole Court) persuaded the City authorities to begin the long process of restoration. A pageant in 1953 entitled *The Three Queens* was the Llandaff Citizens' commemoration of the coronation of Queen Elizabeth II.

'Rookwood' in the 1880s. Built in 1866 by Colonel Sir Edward Stock Hill 'near the old Summer House where Dean Conybeare wrote his sermons, which with the Rookery now form part of the grounds of Rookwood House', it was extended in 1881 by John Prichard. The north lodge and the porte cochère are particularly fine. Early in 1918 it was taken over as an officers' convalescent home, and after the war was purchased by Sir Lawrence Phillips, Bart, MP, and presented to the nation as a home for wounded ex-servicemen for as long as needed, and thereafter for the use of the University of Wales. The bright blue uniforms, white shirts and red ties of 'Rookwood men' were a familiar sight around Llandaff for many years, and the hospital once more received an influx of seriously wounded servicemen during the Second World War. Although the blue uniform has been discontinued it is still Llandaff's pride to support in all possible ways the patients and staff of Rookwood Hospital.

Colonel Sir Edward Stock Hill KCB, MP and his family at Rookwood House, late 1800s. Sir Edward, son of the founder of Hill's Dry Docks in Cardiff, died in 1902 and Lady Hill continued to live there until 1917. A tablet in the Anglican church in Toaramina, Sicily, commemorates 'Miss Mabel Hill, daughter of Sir Edward and Lady Hill of Santa Catarina and Rookwood, Llandaff, born 1860 died 1940.' Miss Hill started a lace school to give local women an interesting occupation, and left the garden of her villa for the benefit of the people of Toaramina, where it is now a public park.

Colonel Sir Edward Stock Hill KCB, MP. Sir Edward, who was born in Bristol in 1834, was for many years associated with the shipbuilding trade in Cardiff and Bristol. He was High Sheriff for the County of Glamorgan in 1885 and was elected as Member of Parliament for the South District of Bristol in 1886.

Rookwood Hospital Staff during the Second World War.

Rookwood Hospital's Occupational Therapy Workshop, demolished in the 1950s.

One of the wards celebrating the Coronation, Rookwood Hospital, 2 June 1953.

St Michael's College, *c.* 1900. When John Prichard died in 1886 he left unfinished the grandly designed expansion of his original 'cottage' on Cardiff Road. The Council of St Michael's Theological College, which had been founded in Aberdare on 1 March 1892 by the generosity of Olivia Emma Talbot, found it convenient to move the College to Llandaff and built on, to the design of F.W. Kempson, a three storey administration block and three residential blocks to form a quadrangle. The building was opened on 8 August 1907 and 32 sets of rooms eventually provided.

St Michael's College 1914-18. During the First World War the College was used by the St John Ambulance Association as a VAD Hospital, as was The Lodge, bought by the College Council as a hostel for students in 1916. The matron was Mrs Wain, who had been the college housekeeper and whose son was posthumously awarded the Victoria Cross in 1917.

St Michael's College rugby football team, 1935. The Warden, Canon E.W. Williamson (later Bishop of Swansea and Brecon), is in the middle of the front row. On his left is the Chaplain, the Revd H. Bowen Evans.

Rebuilding at St Michael's College, 1955. On 2 January 1941, a few hours after the Cathedral had been hit, a land mine struck the south west corner of the quadrangle, demolishing the Chaplain's house and two of the residential blocks. No one was injured, but the buildings were uninhabitable and the new term found the College evacuated to St Davids, where it spent the rest of the war. In October 1945 it returned to Llandaff but to the Bishop's Palace, vacated by American troops. The rebuilding of the western and the administrative blocks, shown here, was not completed until 1956. Margaret Jones, wife of the Chaplain, the Revd Owain Jones, is pictured here with her son Mark, and Susan and Catherine Davies.

St Michael's College at Llys Esgob, 1953-54. From left to right, back row: E.J. Jones, D.B. Bevan, A.G. Lee, C.M. Semper, E.A. Essery, J.M.C. Harries, C.E. Jones, W.P.S. Davies, J.H. Rees, F.V. Stephens. Middle row: F.M.J. Evans, G.E. Williams, F.M. Griffiths, J.A. Ainsley, D.A.H. Jones, C.W.G. Morgan, D. Francis, R.V. Byles, D.G. Brunning. Front row: C. Williams, D. Davies, E.J. Gordon, D.B. Cound, Revd Martin M. Bowen (Sub Warden), Very Revd Eryl S. Thomas (Warden), Revd Owain W. Jones (Chaplain), D. Richards, L.P. Jones, F.G. Turner, A. Loveluck.

Laying the foundation stone of the chapel, designed by George Pace, St Michael's College, 1956. Mark Jones, the Chaplain's son, and Ursula Bowen, the Sub-Warden's daughter, pass the stone to the Warden, the Revd John Charles.

Eight

The Old Parish

The ancient Parish of Llandaff covered an area five times greater than it does today. Along the east bank of the Taff it included parts of the present Llandaff North up to the Pineapple Inn and southwards to the present day Maindy Stadium, including Llys Talybont. To the west it incorporated all of Fairwater and old Ely village as far as the junction between Cowbridge Road and Caerau Lane, where a surviving milestone bears the legend 'Landaff Parish'. To the south it encompassed most of Canton, the old Grange Farm - now Grangetown - and extended to the sea at the far end of what is now Ferry Road.

View north-west up the River Taff at Llandaff, June 1787.

A late nineteenth century view of Llandaff Bridge, looking south. The bridge was built in 1770 by Thomas Roberts. Viewed from what is now Hailey Park, the Cathedral spire can be seen at the extreme left, and above the bridge the chimneys of Baynton House are just discernable. The open field to the right was later developed as 'Highfields'.

Llandaff Bridge from up-stream, late nineteenth century. The River Taff above Llandaff weir has long been a popular stretch of water for rowing. Llandaff weir, in addition to its primary purpose of feeding water to Llandaff's mills, also provided the longest reach of navigable non-tidal water on the Taff. Over the years this stretch has attracted various boating clubs who have established their headquarters on the western bank, both above and below the bridge.

Opposite: Llandaff Bridge from the Llandaff side, late nineteenth century. Development in Llandaff Yard (Llandaff North) initially sprang up along the line of the Glamorganshire Canal, but as can be seen, substantial further building took place during the latter part of the nineteenth century.

Llandaff Bridge, 1970s. The narrow eighteenth century bridge was totally unsuited to the demands of late nineteenth century traffic and a wider bridge deck with unsightly iron latticework parapets was built over the old arches in the early 1890s. The floods of 27 December 1979 so undermined the piers of this bridge that a replacement single span steel structure was installed downstream and the old bridge demolished, only its abutments remaining. The history of the small ruined building alongside the bridge is not known.

Llandaff weir. This weir was designed to allow a take-off of water through the Mill Stream to drive both the corn mill and the tucking mill.

Winter on the River Taff. The 1890s saw a number of very severe winters, one being sufficiently hard to allow skating on the river between the weir and Llandaff Bridge. The replacement parapet and bridge deck can be clearly seen.

All Saints Church, Llandaff North, *c.* 1890. The same hard winter produced this snowbound view of the church.

All Saints Church, Llandaff North, pre-1914. Built in 1890 to the design of Kempson and Fowler at a cost of £1,819, the church was consecrated on 28 January 1891 by Bishop Lewis. It was enlarged in 1914 by the addition of a north aisle and vestries, and the extension of the nave westwards.

All Saints Church choir, August 1914.

All Saints Church, Llandaff North. During the evening of 2 January 1941, in the course of the same air raid which was to wreck Llandaff Cathedral, incendiary bombs set fire to All Saints Church, which was reduced to a shell. The church bell which had been cast for Llandaff Cathedral in 1727, and which had been given to the newly built All Saints in 1890, melted.

Below Mynachdy Lock, Glamorganshire Canal. Lock No 48 on the Glamorganshire Canal lay just south of Western Avenue, adjacent to the traffic lights at the turning to the new Co-op supermarket. The barges were, of course, normally horse-drawn.

Gabalva Cottages, Glamorganshire Canal. This row of canal-side cottages stood in the middle of what is now the Gabalfa estate.

118

Fairwater Road, Llandaff.

Fairwater Road, pre-1936. Looking westward from its junction with Cardiff Road before the building of Nos 6-16 Fairwater Road, but showing the entrance to The Avenue at the lamppost on the right. Almost all the walls and buildings shown here, together with many of the trees, disappeared when Fairwater Road was dramatically widened in the 1960s as housing development in north Fairwater produced an ever increasing volume of traffic.

12. - Fairwater Road, Llandaff

A. M. Lewis (Copyright)

Fairwater Road, pre-1936, looking eastward from the entrance to 'Rookwood', with the entrances to 'The Hermitage' and 'Trenewydd' on the right. The houses of Cardiff Road are just discernible.

The Spreading Chestnut, Fairwater.

Fairwater. At several places around Fairwater and St Fagans the trunks of the trees were banked to make convenient resting places. Here on Fairwater Green there was one at the junction between Plasmawr Road, on the right, and St Fagans Road off to the left.

Miss Florence Osborne beneath the chestnut tree, Fairwater in 1919. The outbuildings of Brook Farm are in the background.

Swiss Cottage, Fairwater. Later known as The Smithy, Swiss Cottage was built by the architect G.E. Halliday in the late 1890s, under the influence of the Arts and Crafts Movement. It was half-timbered, with mullioned windows and flagged floors. The barley-sugar twist chimneys were shipped to the United States when the cottage was demolished in 1972. To the right, across Plasmawr Road, stood Brook Farm. A neatly thatched haystack can be seen beside Swiss Cottage.

Fairwater Green. The felling of the chestnut tree made way for a safer road junction as motor traffic increased.

Brook Farm, 1890. This farm, demolished after the Second World War, had many ancient features; the photograph shows that the left hand section was thatched.

Brook Farm. The thatch is seen more clearly in this early postcard. The novelty of a photographer in this sleepy village has attracted a woman and baby from Brook Farm and a number of curious children who stood in the road, one with a baby in a high perambulator and others grouped around a handcart.

Brook Farm. Spanning the brook in front of Brook Farm stood a wooden hut where Mr Thorn, the farmer, cooled his milk churns.

This thatched farmhouse on the other side of the Green belonged to Mr Cartwright, after whom the lane is named. It was subsequently sold to the Conservative Club and later bought by Brain's Brewery as a public house – the Fairwater Hotel.

In the Dell, now part of Fairwater Park, the Thorns of Brook Farm still used horse power between the two world wars.

Glan-y-Nant Cottage, post-Second World War. Beyond the garden of the cottage stand outbuildings of the house used by the Reardon Smith Nautical College, now a hall of residence for the South Glamorgan Institute of Higher Education. In the years following the Second World War, Anderson shelters were often recycled as garden sheds! Fairwater Health Centre now stands on the site of the cottage.

Llandaff School for the Deaf and Dumb, 1899. This school was founded by Alexander Melville in 1862 and was based initially for a brief period in Landscape Place; it moved to Romilly Crescent in 1865. This photograph of the staff and the pupils was taken in the school garden.

Headstone on Alexander Melville's grave. Melville, who died on 18 April 1891, was buried in the north churchyard of Llandaff Cathedral. The carving above the inscription is a very good likeness of the man who is shown surrounded by his pupils as he teaches them the sign language for 'Jesus'.

Victoria Park. Llandaff Common which included a natural pond fed by streams from the north, was reduced in size and enclosed as a public pleasure ground in 1897 to commemorate Queen Victoria's Diamond Jubilee. The pond was 'formalised', and in more recent years converted into a paddling pool. A bandstand, drinking fountain and a small zoo were features of the new park.

Llandaff from the air, mid-1920s. Although at first glance the centre of the old City looks very much as it is some seventy years later, many changes both great and small can be detected. The most striking is the almost total absence of traffic, only one car being apparent. The site of the shops on the western side of High Street was still an open space fronted by hoardings and the Prichard school was in its heyday. To the extreme left, against the west wall of Penpentre, the terrace of tiny cottages known as Vokes Row still stood. The War Memorial, newly completed, stands out. One can but wonder how the City of Llandaff will change in the next seventy years.

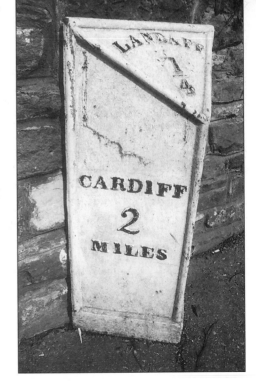

Llandaff's a City,
Cardiff's a Town,
Llandaff shall stand
When Cardiff is drowned.
Old Rhyme

127

Acknowledgements

The Llandaff Society is very grateful to Matthew Williams, Keeper of the Collections at Cardiff Castle, for writing the introduction; we thank Simon Eckley of the Chalford Publishing Company for his help and guidance. The Society is particularly grateful to the Dean and Chapter of Llandaff for allowing access to the Cathedral archives, and to Jill and Nevil James, the Cathedral archivists, without whose commitment and expertise this book could not have been completed. The help of the Local Studies Department of South Glamorgan County Library and of the Glamorgan Record Office is also much appreciated.

Welcome help and the loan of photographs came from a number of people,
to whom we are very grateful, whether or not their photographs were actually included in the
final selection for this volume. In particular we thank:

Aerofilms of Borehamwood (p. 127); All Saints Church, Llandaff North (p. 117);
Jean Amphlett (pp. 14, 15a, 24a, 39b, 52a); Cathedral Archives (pp. 2, 6, 8, 11b, 18a,
20a, 25a, 26b, 27b, 31b, 32b, 77, 79, 80, 81b, 82a, 83a, 84, 85a, 88, 89, 90, 91b, 92b, 112b,
113, 115, 116); Isabel Clark (pp. 22, 25b, 26a, 86a, 105b); Bill Clarke; Mr Cottam, Llandaff
RFC (p. 70a); Norman Cunningham (p. 97); Lisbeth David (pp. 53a, 54, 76, 109a);
Dr Chrystal Davies (pp. 18b, 72a, 85b, 87, 120a, 121b, 122a, 123a, 124); Cyril Davies
(pp. 37, 103); Mary Edge; Margaret Edwards (p. 96b); Heather Elliot (p. 98); George Evans
(pp. 17a, 19b, 27a, 41a, 86b); Mrs V. Evans, Llandaff Citizens Association (pp. 75b, 104b);
Jane Fitz, Headmistress, Howell's School (pp. 48, 49, 50); Glamorgan Record Office
(pp. 67, 99b); Lindsay Gray, Headmaster, The Cathedral School (pp. 45, 46a);
Karen Hamnett; Anne Hann, Cardiff Institute of Higher Education, Llandaff (pp. 64, 65);
J.D. Hine, Llandaff Rowing Club (pp. 68, 69b); John James (p. 93); Mary James (p. 92a);
Nevil & Jill James (pp. 10, 11a, 12a, 13, 16, 17b, 19a, 23b, 24b, 30, 36b, 39a, 52b, 53b, 56,
57b, 58, 63b, 69a, 74b, 82b, 83b, 94b, 108b, 111, 112a, 114b, 119, 120b, 121a, 125b, 126);
Mrs Ginny Jenkins, Rookwood Hospital (pp. 106b, 107); Huw John (p. 51b); Barbara Jones;
Margaret Jones (pp. 38b, 40a, 110); Norman Jones (p. 114a); Mrs Kennet & Mrs Daphne
Morgan, Elm Tree House School (p. 47); David Lewis, Llandaff; David Lewis,
STP Photography (p. 92b); Mrs M.J. Lewis (pp. 32b, 33, 95b, 96a); Llandaff Society
(pp. 9, 15b, 23a, 28a, 36a, 41b, 60a, 62a, 108a); Joyce Lloyd (p. 51b); Anne Matthews,
Rookwood Hospital: Miss Margaret Morgan; Mrs Mary Morgan (pp. 46b, 81a, 95a, 100, 101);
Geoff North (pp. 58b, 122b); Fred Pollard (p. 91a); Dennis Pope (p. 60b);
Ruth Powell (pp. 12b, 34, 71b, 94a, 123b); Sheila Pym (pp. 40b, 42a, 72b, 73, 104a, 109b);
Stephen Rowson (pp. 59b, 71a, 102a, 118); Margaret Samuel (pp. 38a, 42b, 70b, 74a);
Joan Serjent; Ruth Skye (p. 31a); South Glamorgan County Library (pp. 20b, 21, 28b, 35,
57a, 66a, 125a); Heather Stephens (p. 66b); Matthew Williams (pp. 102b, 105a, 106a);
Beryl Withyman (pp. 62b, 63a).
The attributes 'a' (above) and 'b' (below) refer to the position of the photograph on each
particular page.
Our thanks are also extended to any others who have helped with this volume
but who are not named above.

The following members of the Llandaff Society
worked on the production of the book:
Norman Cunningham, Lisbeth David, Chrystal Davies, Jill James, Nevil James.